Yes!
You can have a
HAPPY MARRIAGE!

*Effective Strategies to Make Time
for What Matters Most to You*

Table of Contents

Acknowledgements

With everything we do all Glory and Honor is to our Lord and Savior Jesus Christ.

We are ever so grateful that the Lord has graced us with the gift of our marriage and the gift of each other. We have truly embraced 'a threefold cord is not easily broken.'

Michael and Carolyn Byrd

Introduction

18 Then the Lord God said, "It is not good for the man
to be alone. I will make a helper
who is just right for him."
- Genesis 2:18 (NLT)

We live in a world covered in the omnipresence of God Almighty, a world that God Himself eloquently spoke into existence, a universe that was perfectly formed from the His very mind.

He made man from the earth and breathed His Spirit into him to give life. Man, alone, enjoyed the sweet fellowship with God, the long walks across the glistening streams talking, the nights spent under the moonlight conversing about his day.

This was the ultimate relationship; man shared his thoughts with God, man beheld what no other creature shared - identity. Man was the only species given the gift of representing God, he was created in the image and likeness of God.

The Alpha Himself endowed man with His vision, the vision that of a perfect being, free from sin. Man was mirrored after the reflection of God, giving man the ability to contain the pure essence of God. His essence is pictured in man, having the capacity and authority to speak the existence of things that had not yet appeared, having the wisdom to offer peace, having the nature to bring healing, having the strength to provide, what an awesome gift given to man!

 Yet Elohim, the creator of Man, said 'It is not good for man to be alone. I will make a helper who is just right for him."

From there, the first surgery known to this world, without anesthesia, scalpel or stitches, took place. God gently put man to rest, removed a rib from his body, and created the ultimate helpmate. From the moment Adam, the first man, laid his eyes on her, he called her "Bone of my bone; flesh of my flesh". Her title from that moment was "Woman" - man with a womb.

 Why would God create man as an individual then say it's not good for him to be alone? The answer is very simple.

The one who **completed** him was **already a part** of him. When God created man, everything that would **complete** man was made with him, and contained in him.

God reached into the depth of man's being, brought out the best part of him, and presented her to him in a package that would arouse his curiosity and satisfied his desire. It was in the presence of this union that God declared His elation with His creation, the first instituted marriage as He stood and declared the anointing of increase and multiplication shall cover this union.

DIMENSION ONE
"In the Beginning"

Michael and Carolyn Byrd

Chapter 1

Contract or Covenant?

M arriage is a biblical covenant which allows two people to be unconditionally joined together in all areas of life, from the physical to the spiritual. Marriage is the one place we find blessings and honor molded together not just for the purpose of bringing glory to God, but for the unison of humanity to experience the union of fellowship in one exclusive love.

The Webster's New World Dictionary defines "covenant" as a binding and solemn agreement to do or keep from doing a specified thing. It also defines the term "contract" also as an agreement between people especially formally set forth in writing and enforceable by law.[1]

Simply put, if the **one** thing that keeps a husband or wife in marriage is in written form, **it's a contract** however, contracts can be broken and rewritten to suit one's needs. In a contract one can re-negotiate the terms.

---

[1] Webster's New World College Dictionary 4th edition

In a contract, people live by a silent code and follow every letter of the law; if it's written on the paper, then the people are meant to abide by the rules and regulations. Conversely, a contract can be one's personal discretion. If the written binding agreement is exposed to heat, water, sharp items or has an expiration date, your mutual agreement in the marriage can be destroyed! This alone should show you that the perception of marriage as "contractual" does **not** align with God's initial intention for the institution

UNDERSTANDING A COVENANT

The first question a married couple should ask themselves is, "Do we understand what a covenant is?"

Another question to consider is, "Do we value our marriage as a covenant under God?"

The entire concept of the Bible is based upon covenant which can be translated into a strong, irreversible agreement. A covenant is a foundational word that speaks the embodiment of the emotions, character and mind of God.

When God is willing to share whatever may be on His heart one will immediately note the indication of His extending Himself to willfully engage in a covenant relationship with mankind.

Two of God's greatest desires are that we share the same feelings with Him, and that we also share those feelings with one another, more seen in a covenant marriage. This gives understanding as to why marriage is honorable before God.

A covenant is **not** something that comes along after you find the spouse of your choice. We have been introduced to the concept of a covenant from the moment we entered fellowship with God. A covenant is already programmed inside of you, placed there by God. God will allow the ideal person to enter in your life. At the onset of the meeting the reserved passion and love that was secretly stored in you begins to flow out towards your mate naturally. A covenant is never to be taken lightly; God views them will all seriousness and gravity.

In biblical days, a breach of a covenant was grounds for death. Take a look at the story of Jonathan, the son of Saul, who betrayed his father to keep his covenant with David.[2] A biblical covenant was often sealed by the shedding of blood. Without this ceremonial act, the Bible states there is no remission of sin. [3] The covenant was paramount in the biblical era, and it should be taken with the same gravity now.

For all intents and purposes, we can look at the process of a woman's hymen being broken. Here, the shedding of blood is symbolically viewed as the sharing of the blood covenant between that man and that woman. A covenant was imperative then and continues to be crucial now.

---

[2] 1Samuel 20.

[3] Hebrews 9:22).

Covenant identifies covering

A covenant requires an agreement shared between two or more parties. In a Christian context, a covenant has God's covering. A covering is simply something that lays over or is wrapped around a thing for concealment, protection or warmth.[4]

When God covers his people, he lavishes his love and provisional care, which brings about unshakeable peace.God is a true example of what a covering should be. This must be emulated within a marriage. Below is a vow that is made between spouses.

This is a vow of covering made from a husband to his wife:

With everything inside me, I am willing to wrap you in my arms with care. I will take my coat and envelope you when you're cold. I vow to take the cold, as long as you are warm.

I will take the pain so that you can be free. I will conceal you and protect you from any sign of danger. I promise to protect, shield and guard you with all my heart. I will embrace what embraces you, and put myself against all who put themselves against you.

I will camouflage myself over you, so that I can absorb whatever tries to attack you. I will contend with those who contend with you.

While reflecting on what a covering *is,* let us now expound on what it *is not.*

---

[4] dictionary.com

A covering is *not:*

- A person void of the ability to honor, love, cherish, and respect another.

- A person whose mindset is consumed with self and therefore leaves their spouse as a secondary thought.

- A person who refuses to work and provide for the family or place his or her needs before the needs of the family.

- A person who is unstable or inconsistent in all or any of their ways.

- A physical, psychological, or verbal abuser.

As you see, there are many facets on what a covering is **not.**

One must search within the depths of his or her heart to make determine if they truly understand what a covering is.

If at any given moment one or more have been out of balance, time is still waiting for the adjustment to take place. Remember it's never too late.

Covenant identifies commitment

A covenant is not for the uncommitted. It is an agreement that requires extensive commitment.

Are you willing to be extensively committed to your life mate forever?

Many people have a hard time, with the word "commitment", and it seems to be more for the men than women. In many instances, men are surrounded by insufficient role models in their singleness and this imposes and reinforces the fear. This fear could paralyze a man, ultimately preventing him from having a truly monogamous relationship.

Commitment means that one vows and promises to be obligated to the other for the rest of their lives. They exclusively belong to one and not another.

These words can be intimidating if one has never shared anything with others. To some, commitment can resemble bondage, imprisonment, financial struggle, or even a no-win situation.

Commitment, however, is none of those things.

The cultural belief system one may have, may not have embraced this word called commitment. Maybe, the examples around you may have not lived the perfect example in front of you.

Today is the day to wipe away all the preconceived notions that have taken up your mind, and have now become seeds for infidelity.

It's time to take a new picture of commitment and let it start with God. Let it flow to the heart and soul of you and your spouse.

Become the new picture for the people around you and the generations after you. Readjust the lens once looked through and focus on a fresh new beginning. This could be the time that your marriage becomes the model for the word commitment because the strength of one's marriage lies in the foundation of its covenant.

Become the example in which others may live by and children could model.

Covenant identifies connection

In order to feel a strong relationship connection there must be a covenant powerful enough to connect the two.

For example, the Bible speaks of how Ruth was connected to Naomi; proof that the power of a covenant can beyond friendship. It reaches to the soul of a matter. Ruth's mind, will and emotions came into a divine alignment, thereby causing her to make a conscious decision that would lead her to her destiny.

A covenant involves the soul of a man/woman, who both have a freewill choice in the matter. In a marriage one must bring his/her mind in direct alignment with the heart, for if at any time one is out of order it will have an adverse effect on the marriage.

In the end it was the covenant that Ruth held with Naomi that connected her to her blessing. It was through Naomi's guidance that Ruth was able to connect with and eventually marry Boaz.

Covenant connections should only be with people who have like passions desires, feelings, and destiny. Without such a connection in your heart and mind, a marriage will not grow.

It is through the association of husband and wife with God and through that relationship connection, God will bless. Being in a covenant connection with your spouse has great benefits for both it's as if God creates a way to get the greatest happiness to both individuals through his law of opportunity.

Chapter 2

The Elements of Destruction

Heat is considered a form of energy existing as the result of the random motion of molecules and is the form of energy that is transferred between bodies as a result of their temperature difference.[5]

The husband and wife are two individuals with two distinct ideals. Two different opinions, individually reared with different upbringing values.

At any given moment something can spark negative energy between them and cause a sudden rise of temperature causing heated differences. If it is not handled with careful efficiency, the sudden rise of the heat can begin to burn out of control and cause major catastrophic damage.

This sudden rise of heat is the result of remaining in amalgamated tension, where no one wanted to yield, and both desired to have his/her way.

---

[5]Webster's New World College Dictionary

Consider the fact that you will not always see eye to eye, but both have a right to see. If it becomes a norm to take away the right of the other, heat will rise quickly.

Road rage is a serious problem, and sadly not all the drivers caught in such a vent is aggressive drivers. Some are drivers who get fed up with the torment and finally snap in the heat of the moment, this most certainly does not justify or validates an excuse to vent or blow up.

When little sparks are not smothered out they will turn into burning flames. Perhaps the heat could have been handled before the damage, but that happens only when both husband and wife understands that each has an opinion, and both must learn to agree to disagree.

In a **contract** once the sparks begin it's easy to walk away never to return. In a **covenant** the couple seeks help to put out the sparks before they become burning flames of destruction. Collateral damage is irreversible.

The force of water

Water damage can occur within a marriage because of an unstable foundation which was built with a faulty system designed for failure which ultimately leads to divorce.

The force of water is tremendous; it often comes in great amounts causing damage and destruction. These great waves of water or floods have many causes.

Cause No. 1: The atmosphere in a home has become a climate of little to no communication which causes a shift and drops the warmth in any relations. The home that once was warm and inviting has turned into an empty cold shell.

Is your marriage water proof?

Yes, one may have been married for some years and have endured the long days of non-communication. The marriage has been unattended or unoccupied and without passionate heat for long periods of time.

When this occurs one spouse tends to deny the other because of a systematic breakdown. Frozen pipes can cause irreversible damage!

Cause No. 2: Your marriage could be suffering from back-ups, which has caused a flooding in your foundation.

When was the last time you complimented your spouse?

When was the last time you went on a spontaneous date just the two of you?

Does your marriage have enough assurance to weather the storms?

Storms are the things that drain your marriage from the outside.

It's important to express kind gestures to your spouse. The pressures of life can be overwhelming and just taking a break can aide in the longevity of life and marriage. Your spouse needs your personal time and endorsements to survive in world filled with struggle, pain or disappointments.

Water damage begins subtly, and can go unnoticed for a while. As the water begins to pour in, it rises and can cause the most unsightly defacement.

Water can enter in the best of marriages but if the marriage is founded on a contract then the incentive to care for this problem will become minimal. This will lead to a need of tearing down and gutting out or to permanent destruction to a marriage.

The razor sharp tongue

There are three words to best describe the word "sharp", (1) abrupt (2) harsh or intense (3) sarcastic[6]

It is imperative that all choices of words are considered, especially in the presence of a communication breakdown.

"Whatever comes up comes out", without any regards towards the feelings of another. Once the trigger has been pulled with the tongue there is no retraction. The damage is inevitable.

> [21] *Death and life are in the power of the tongue, and*
> *they who indulge in it shall eat the fruit of it*
> *[for death or life].*
> **- Proverbs 18:21 (AMP)**

---

[6] Webster's New World Pocket Dictionary 4th addition 2000, Merriam Webster's Pocket Dictionary New Edition 2006

Words can kill! Too many of the wrong words can damage a marriage. The tongue is a sharp item and can be used as a deadly weapon, words have definite power and lasting effects.

Words have the power to hurt the toughest people. They are not easily forgotten.

> [1] *A gentle answer turns away wrath, but harsh words*
> *cause quarrels.*
> **- Proverbs 15:1 (TLB)**

It's all in the way one receives, *then* answer, it takes two to argue no one can successfully argue alone. It's usually not the sender who ignites the blaze of an argument, but the responder.

The responder has to make a quick conscious decision to appease the situation, or make it worse. In making the choice to redirect it turns the potential argument away from into a peaceful situation. But if the responders takes hold of the bait, and responds with aggression, this will most certainly ignite a quarrel.

In a contract, once little fires began to stir it leads to a bush fire in which there's nothing left to do but vacate.

But a marriage in a **covenant** *has a "no evacuation clause". In a covenant instead of the heat causing combustions, it is used as a vehicle to stir up a greater passion to press on.*

Private Struggles become Public Shame:

*22 There is nothing covered which will not be seen
openly, and nothing has been made secret
which will not come to light.*
- Mark 4:22 (BBE)

Many times couples secretly harbor frustration and denial of the struggles that grip their everyday home life.

Many people become absorbed in the pain of their relationship to cover and protect the one whom they pledged to have and to hold. Behind closed doors true love does not flow, respect is a short lived term that does not visit the home. Virtue is part of the past, desire has long left the scene, the one whose words stimulated the emotions of the heart, has now become the trigger of pain. All the things that once ignited the flame has become the torch of sorrow driven by a rage and anger.

Could one reason why many take the behind the doors verbal abuse and disrespect, is to protect the image of their marriage and the image of the spouse? If this is not dealt with, and help is not sought, what is done in the dark will show up in the light.

A continuation to mask the truth that something is wrong, or protecting a reputation will only leads to more destruction. Loving one in public should be a result of loving one in private.

The eyes are the open windows to what's really housed in the heart; if love is present love will come forth. A term that we often use is "if it's in you, it must come out" good or bad it will shine forth.

Whatever one chooses not to deal with, will manifest in time, if the marriage is going through rough times seek help, before the cord begins to unwind.

Before a marriage takes a wrong turn the warning signs emerge, but is anyone listening. Seeking the counsel of a marriage counselor or spiritual leader is not a shameful event it becomes the first step towards restoration and the saving of the marriage.

This should not be a forced meeting it most certainly should be a mutual understanding as to where and whom the couple will confide. Seek an unbiased counsel one whom both trust will be advantageous to all.

A marriage should always bring God glory, it's radiant glow always tell the true story.

Time: The lost commodity

Time is a precious commodity given to mankind, yet it is also the most disrespected and neglected. A marriage should never grow old and undesirable if the most precious of all gifts was handled with care, *time*. Time is a marker which marks the beginning, memories, dreams, adventures, decisions, joys, and pain. If one takes the time to cultivate and discover the beauty of marriage, then marriage will stand the test of time. A spouse gets out what they put in and time marks the spot and will serve as an indicator of what has been instituted. Make the best of your time together and time will make its mark with remarkable longevity.

Going back to the original question, how well is your understanding of a covenant?

By now you should have a clearer insight of a covenant and can offer a clear concise statement about what you have gained. Whether it has become a new awareness or an addition to the knowledge that you have previously attained the surety should lie in the fact that your marriage is one of covenant.

Take time now to *meditate* on the things you have read, *evaluate* where you are in your relationship, if change is needed began today making covenant a priority and reestablishing a new foundation on which your marriage is built.

Remember, time has no boundaries and sets new opportunities to begin anew, it's never too late to realize that you're always entering a new beginning, and with this new beginning you can have a working knowledge and understanding the word covenant.

Chapter 3

The Mystery of Marriage

So is marriage a covenant?

Yes.

The institution of marriage is a divine picture of Christ and His Bride.

In addition, the Bible speaks of marriage to us as the mystery of Deity. Marriage itself relates to a deeply spiritual union.

In a marriage, the wife can be likened to the Holy Spirit, and the man to the Word of God. It takes both to produce.

This is clearly illustrated in Paul's church to Ephesus:

> *25 Husbands, love your wives, as Christ loved the church and gave Himself up for her, 26 So that He might sanctify her, having cleansed her by the washing of water with the Word, 27 That He might present the church to Himself in glorious splendor, without spot or wrinkle or any such things [that she*

might be holy and faultless]. [28] *Even so husbands*
should love their wives as [being in a sense] their
own bodies. He who loves his own wife loves himself.
[29] *For no man ever hated his own flesh, but nourishes*
and carefully protects and cherishes it, as Christ does
the church, [30] *Because we are members (parts) of His*
body. [31] *For this reason a man shall leave his father*
and his mother and shall be joined to his wife, and the
two shall become one flesh. [32] *This mystery is very*
great, but I speak concerning [the relation of] Christ
and the church. [33] *However, let each man of you*
[without exception] love his wife as [being in a sense]
his very own self; and let the wife see that she
respects and reverences her husband [hat she notices
him, regards him, honors him, prefers him, venerates,
and esteems him; and hat she defers to him, praises
him, and loves and admires him exceedingly].
- Ephesians 5:25-33 (AMP)

Marriage is spiritual. It is a mystery which is likened to the covenant of Christ and His church, and it's *likened to* the relationship of the Holy Spirit and the Word.

The Holy Spirit is gentle but full of power. The Holy Spirit is a comforter who gives revelation, insight and knowledge. But, he does not function of his own, without the Word. The Holy Spirit is liken unto the wife and the Word is liken the husband. They are two distinct beings yet they are one, one without the other would leave one void.

There is an intimate relationship between the Holy Spirit and The Word, together when both are realized and respected there is the most exasperating experience known to mankind.

The husband must tap into the inner recesses of his wife to reach into the depths of her soul, that they may become one as was instituted by the Father. Even as the Holy Spirit is required to usher one into the very presence of God, the wife is necessary to birth the dreams and visions of her husband. A word without the spirit is just a word, but the word with the spirit becomes a powerful explosion climaxing into the most wonderful intimate relationship between man and woman.

The marriage covenant is a threefold cord.

⁹ Two can accomplish more than twice as much as one, for the results can be much better. ¹⁰ If one falls, the other pulls him up; but if a man falls when he is alone, he's in trouble. ¹¹ Also, on a cold night, two under the same blanket gain warmth from each other, but how can one be warm alone? ¹² And one standing alone can be attacked and defeated, but two can stand back-to-back and conquer; three is even better, for a triple-braided cord is not easily broken.
- Ecclesiastes 4:9-12 (TLB)

One cord can be stretched easily and torn apart; two cords would insure more strength; but three cords woven together could not be easily broken.

The two together in marriage, working for the same results has a better chance at achieving those results, than one who has to strive alone. Now when a third cord is added it triples the results of strength.

The third cord is in your belief, your trust, that you are not alone in your marriage, but there is a force greater than the two of you. The presence of God in your marriage is the cord that keeps your marriage strong. The third cord is the electricity that sends the surge of power to increase the love. It's the umbilical cord that keeps you together even when you are apart. It's the belt that keeps you secure and tightly fastened together when you want to jump ship. It's the fine fabric that knits you together that never runs or get tired of being connected. It's the volume that speaks when the words cannot properly form in one's mouth that expresses the deep feelings in one's heart. A marriage is as strong as the third cord it's in twinned with, the strength of your marriage lies in the strength of your third cord.

For there are three that bear record in heaven, the
Father, the Word, and the Holy Ghost: and
these three are one.
- 1 John 5:7 (KJV) [7]

The strength of the marriage is in direct relation to the silent but yet vocal, the unseen but yet visible, the untouchable but yet tangible. He's the most important ingredient whose always there but never intrusive. As the three bear record in heaven the three bear record in marriage, for the three are one just as the two become one. For understanding of this spiritual expression one must return to biblical foundation which is the alpha of all things.

Marriage the most sacred of covenants.

When Eve is presented before Adam, we hear Adam say, "This is now bone of my bones, and flesh of my flesh; she shall be called woman, because she was taken out of man."
- Genesis 2:23

This shows the exceptional way the Lord sees the woman, she is seen as man's gift. Every woman is designed to be a gift to some man, but she is ultimately a gift from the Lord. The gift is to be cherished, loved, and cared for, when a gift such as she is presented to a man it has been handed to him as an everlasting gift to be adored.

Marriage is a binding love of commitment which cherishes the precious gift that God has graced one with and holding on to it until there is no more life in it. In marriage vows these words, "to have and to hold 'til death do we part", are repeated robotically and many have never examined its meaning.

Its covenantal meaning is that one promises to take the other as his/her spouse that they would take the good and rough that comes with becoming the others' mate. A mutual agreement between both of taking the responsibility to stay connected through life's challenges, weathering the storms, protecting the investment, sifting through changes, and maintaining the integrity of the marriage until life leaves one of the two.

It's repeated but is it reality? The answer is it's only as real as the perceptional images engraved in one's mind. *Selah*

DIMENSION TWO
"Understanding your spouse"

Michael and Carolyn Byrd

Chapter 1

Optical Illusions

OUTSIDE LOOKING IN

Often, we gain the understanding of marriage through the eyes of personal opinion which can be translated as a one dimensional plane.

Even with the natural eye there are three dimensions from which we capture what we see to make one visual picture. We see in stages however the brain has a way of bringing what we see into focus so that one may see a multiple of things as a single completed picture.

One must marvel at how God made a small member of the human body equally as important as the rest of the anatomy to function in such an intricate way. Man's visual perception of sight is; nearsighted, farsighted intermediate which is your mid-range sight.

A farsighted spouse has the ability to see in the distant future but overlooks what's right in front of them, while the nearsighted spouse can only recognize issues when it becomes up close and personal, their capacity for the seeing past today is a blur.

Most often disagreements occur because of the different dimensions in which the other gathers information which aides in perception. The brain signal the eyes to see and the eye which functions in purpose gathers the various dimension of images to present a whole picture to the brain which responds accordingly.

Seeing through a dimmed picture

Never set your focus on another marriage and set it as a gage for your marriage. One must always remember that you stand on the outside of another couple's relationship looking in which can cause one to have optical illusions. Only the husband or wife knows the truth about their marriage, the one on the outside only thinks it sees inside another marriage. To have an illusion means to have something that deceives the senses or mind, i.e.; by appearing to exist when it does not or appearing to be one thing when it is in fact another. When one sees another marriage that may appear to be solid and what they desire to have they see that marriage on a dimension elevated above their own.

Let's define a marriage dimension - The intense expansion of a marital union extending that union to greater heights of passion by increasing the widths of wisdom thus stimulating communication all while captivating the mind of one's spouse and striving to gain a new perspective of love.

One word of advice is never judge your marriage by the dimension you see another marriage this creates optical illusions, because one is only seeing from one's own perspective. Mistaken sensory perception in psychology is a misinterpretation of an experience of sensory perception, especially a visual one, where the stimuli are objectively present and the mistaken perception is due to physical rather than psychological causes.

Selah moments:

1. Every marriage functions at different levels at varying times, therefore there is no true gage of another marriage whereby there should be any comparison.

2. Mistaken sensory perception can destroy a marriage causing an exposure of dissatisfaction which could take a lifetime to try and overcome and heal.

3. The grass is not always greener in someone else garden it just may be that someone has invested more time which caused a healthy blossoming to occur.

4. Every marriage experiences shifts, good dimensional shifts occur as a result of a vibrant, fresh and stimulating marriage.

1. Please note that every marriage will go through several dimensional shifts, never get comfortable at one dimension because another is possibly on the way.

Chapter 2

The womb of desire

———⋅◦⟨∾⟩◦⋅———

D*esire is an expression of longing for something that brings gratification or pleasure to someone ultimately producing purpose.*

Desire has to become a driving force and the foundation from which to set your expectations high in your marriage. Most people never learn the art of transmitting their strongest emotions (which is desires) into dreams of a constructive nature within their marriage. The enemy of desire is disappointment; any disappointing past experiences generally has the effect of causing loss of interest, depression and thoughts of failure.

Whenever this happens a settlement occurs, one will settle for mediocrity instead of striving to the next dimension in the relationship. Everyone has a need to express their desires; by nature all have desires, and whether they are natural or spiritual, desire is an instrumental factor in a marriage. When the desire is shut off or shut down, people lose their natural ability to dream, without a dream (vision) people perish. Within the marriage union, if one spouse shuts the doors to expression of the others desire, they shut the portals in the conscious mind of that spouse which will release good or bad what was lying dormant in the subconscious mind of their spouse.

Desire is a powerful emotion it is also a womb in the spirit if that womb is block or shut off, it could leave the marriage in a barren state. The marriage will become unfruitful to either one or both spouses and the possibility of never producing to fulfill God's intent will be evident causing one or both to lose their zeal in the marriage.

It is imperative that each spouse empowers the other to pursue their desires, as the couple engages in conversation with each other because of the closeness of intimacy there should most definitely be an automatic mental stimulation that occur.

Desire is the starting point of all achievement within marriage; it should be a foundation on which to build upon. Marriage will always take persistence and perseverance in order to advance to new dimensions of accomplishments. Once both the husband and wife have a definiteness of the purpose for their union together they would unlock the joys of fulfillment and enter into greater dimensions. Both must have a burning desire to possess the dreams hidden within the wombs of their thoughts.

"When one diminishes in desire, one stops dreaming when one stop dreaming then one stops living".

31

Chapter 3

THE WOMB OF THE SOUL
(*mind, will and emotions*)

The "mind" thinks the thoughts that lead to failed or successful marriages!

A mind stretched to a new measurement can never return to the same capacity. Whatever one devotes their attention to can take root in their life. If a person's total focus, thought, and drive is geared around thinking their marriage is a failure, then it give birth to that thought.

If one focuses their thoughts towards believing the marriage is successful, they will manifest that thought. If success is practiced, success is what will be achieved. It's all a matter of thought. Spouses sometimes suffer what we call the rubber band effect thinking. The rubber band effect is what happens when the mind refuses to explore areas of new growth and begins to settle for the fact that the marriage will always remain consistent with its habitual state of lacking innovation and freshness.

Every day's thoughts should be filled with the right things; proper thoughts yield the proper solution. If the thought is erroneous, the solution will be erroneous. The mind is a powerful tool, and should be used effectively within the marriage for the greater purpose of stimulating positive thoughts for a successful future between both individuals.

The "will" incubates what the mind has thought in preparation for delivery of that thought!

Inside the womb of each person male or female there is a constant incubation process occurring. Messages are transported to the incubator or *the will* from the *mind*, the will has the ability to qualify or disqualify the thought. The *will* prepares the thought for delivery then it assumes the role as the umpire having the authority to make the decision to except or condemn what should be passed on to the emotions or dismissed from the mind.

The *will* of two spouses can be diametrically opposed to one another. This can cause problems which we will identify in our next topic "the emotions". The will of each individual should've been discussed prior to entering the marriage union at the formation of the relationship or the "getting to know you" stage.

Problems occur when one spouse is unaware of how strong the other spouse's determination power to complete an obsession actually is. How well do you know your spouse's obsessions motivators and drives for power? Often by the time a situation arises which reflects a person's strong willpower, it's too late to do the research that should've been done in advance. It is the responsibility of each spouse to know your spouse's convictions prior to challenging situations arising and that proactive knowledge gained will yield successful resolution and unification of both individual wills or expectations and ultimately results in the best benefit for the union of the marriage.

The will is the developing place, the brewing place and the gathering strength place for the thoughts! What are some of the recent thoughts relating to your spouse that may have come to your mind? Which of those thoughts are being incubated in your will for presentation and delivery through your emotions?

The "emotions" manifest the incubated thought of the *will* leading to a failed or successful marriage!

Emotions are in the soul realm of a person therefore knowing what's at the seat of their emotions is important. Emotions can be positive or negative within a person. An emotion is a mental state of feelings, thoughts, and behavior.

Emotions are subjective experiences, or experienced from an individual point of view. Emotion is often associated with mood, temperament, personality, and disposition. We can see how knowing a person's will, can help spouses have an advantage of knowing their partners emotions. The emotions are the external fruit of the internal workings. When the emotions are visibly displayed the full manifestation of the secret hidden things good or bad is observed.

Love for a spouse should be first on the mind, incubated in the will, and manifested in your every emotion, and it's this formula that will yield the perfect fruit towards that of a successful marriage.

Negative emotions

Many major decision have been made during the heat of negative emotions, often those decisions have been decisions that many people have grown to regret making even years later, emotions always involve unforeseen circumstances in the future because they have the ability to paint a cloudy or distorted biased picture of a given situation.

A negative emotional person is a self-centered person that refuses to give up their right to be wrong, that person justifies their right to want what they want, making it hard to convince them to compromise, even in matters where situations are open for debate within relationships. Negative emotions cause hurts to the people that are up close and personal so often they're the same people that go unappreciated and uncelebrated.

Negative emotions can leave lasting scars on children that could cause them a lifetime of agony and pain. There are two areas that form the foundation or give us the basis of how we function in our emotional behavior patterns. The first is an *innate behavioral pattern*, meaning existing in one from birth, the second is a *learned behavioral pattern*, meaning acquired by experience. If one or both areas of behavioral patterns are faulty within a parent, then the message gleaned by the children will perpetuate an ongoing cycle of emotional behavioral disorder. One suggested method to help a child of a product of negative innate or learned patterns is to break the cycle of negativity and replace it with positive cycles that would be responsible for cleansing of the mind, will and emotions.

God is the only one that can change our nature denoting character, personality, temperament, disposition, spirit, and make up.

If this has impacted in any way please pause and pray this simple however profound prayer:

God we pray that you would change our minds, to mirror the mind of Christ, our will to reflect the will of God, and our emotions to be ruled by the Holy Spirit, father it is then and only then that the scales of mental and emotional scars can drop off, and the newness of the life can penetrate my very being. Amen!

The mind thinks it, the will incubates it, and the emotions manifest it!

Chapter 4

The power of identity "The Wife"

*22 He who finds a [true] wife finds a good thing
and obtains favor from the Lord.*
- Proverbs 18:22 (AMP)

First we must identify the term "wife" – a married woman – a woman of covenant, a woman who is committed to the life and wellbeing of her husband. She's committed to his vision, his needs, and his desires **along with her own**. She's not single minded in her thinking. The wellbeing of her husband is always on the top of her thoughts. Her dreams are not lost; they are in relation to his vision. For she understands that the moment she says "I do" the two becomes one. A wife has a noble character where her husband never has to question her loyalty because her values and thoughts are always genuine.

*10 "Who can find a wife with a strong character? She
is worth far more than jewels. 11 Her husband trusts
her with {all} his heart, and he does not lack anything
good. 12 She helps him and never harms him all the*

days of her life. [13] *"She seeks out wool and linen {with*
care} and works with willing hands. [14] *She is like*
merchant ships. She brings her food from far away. [15]
She wakes up while it is still dark and gives food to
her family and portions of food to her female slaves.
[16] *"She picks out a field and buys it. She plants a*
vineyard from the profits she has earned. [17] *She puts*
on strength like a belt and goes to work with energy.
[18] *She sees that she is making a good profit. Her lamp*
burns late at night. [19] *"She puts her hands on the*
distaff, and her fingers hold a spindle. [20] *She opens*
her hands to oppressed people and stretches them out
to needy people. [21] *She does not fear for her family*
when it snows because her whole family has a double
layer of clothing. [22] *She makes quilts for herself. Her*
clothes are {made of} linen and purple cloth. [23] *"Her*
husband is known at the city gates when he sits with
the leaders of the land. [24] *"She makes linen garments*
and sells them and delivers belts to the merchants. [25]
She dresses with strength and nobility, and she smiles
at the future. [26] *"She speaks with wisdom, and on her*
tongue there is tender instruction. [27] *She keeps a close*
eye on the conduct of her family, and she does not eat
the bread of idleness. [28] *Her children and her husband*
stand up and bless her. In addition, he sings her
praises, by saying, [29] *'Many women have done noble*
work, but you have surpassed them all!' [30] *"Charm is*
deceptive, and beauty evaporates, {but} a woman who

*has the fear of the Lord should be praised. [31] Reward
her for what she has done, and let her achievements
praise her at the city gates."*
- Proverbs 31:10-31 (GW)

The wife should be an asset, not a liability to her husband, she's a foundation in his life who gives him encouragement. Her faithfulness is proven through her dedication. Many make the mistake in believing that once a woman becomes a bride she becomes a wife, not necessarily so, a bride is for a day, but a wife is a lifetime, sadly marriages have begun under this misconception. Gliding down the aisle does not render one a wife, the mental and spiritual preparation of a wife shapes the character of a woman long before she says "I do".

The idea of becoming a "wife" is a mental concept that resides in the mind of a woman. Therefore when she says "I do" she begins living the life she conditioned by her thoughts. There are no struggles of her identity because her thoughts house the pre-enclosed images of her beliefs. If in the mind of a bride her main objective to being a wife is his name and the entitlement of what he owns; the life with that bride will be just that. Name only, no substance or value, just the title.

But if the bride's preconceived thoughts of a wife is similar to that of which is stated in the previous paragraph, this bride will be an assets as a wife to her husband. This does not mean she's prefect, it means she understands and is focused on her purpose for being a part of his life fulfilling her design and intention. A wife is more than a title it's a state of mind with direction.

[14] House and wealth are a heritage from fathers, but a
wife with good sense is from the Lord.
*- **Proverbs 19:14 (BBE)***

This is a wife with good understanding; she identifies and fulfills her role in the marriage. Her life is governed by a mutual submission in which she postures herself accordingly. The wisdom of her understanding is not one of bondage it's one of beauty the result of her freedom of choice. Submission is always a decision that must be decided by the one who chooses to submit. The beauty of submission is that it gives both ways.

Her perception of her life is that of value and substance. The wife who knows the value of her worth understands the submission of such value is as unto the Lord will produce a far greater reward of glory. After all she becomes her husband crown of glory; the splendor of his thoughts, the mark of his distinction and the symbol of his favor. She complements her husband with her poised character and presence. She personifies his power and authority in the earth realm unequivocally she's graced as his queen due to God's organization of the universe, man is the ruler and woman is the ruling queen by his side. This woman undoubtedly acknowledges and lives in her value of a wife.

Are you sure?

To be sure is to be free from doubt, to be confident, to be fully persuaded, to be positive, and never disappointing to oneself or others. This is the depiction of stability with an assurance of certainty beyond question. This is a woman who refuses to question her value or worth, her identity is locked in her thoughts not the opinion of others. Her dreams are as a result of the visions of herself, therefore she there is not room in the consciousness of her thoughts for negative thoughts of herself. She measures her success by her Self and no one else, knowing that the sureness of herself worth produces a security that leads to her destiny. A sure woman sees no barriers for she knows that the only barriers in her life or her marriage are the ones she sets for herself. Destiny is the result of a pursue, pursue traveled from the road positive thought, positive thoughts originated from the mind of security.

When the course of a wife's journey to destiny is strong, everything she does add worth to her marriage. The sureness of her purpose creates a security in their marriage. A woman who struggles within herself creates a burden to her husband. Insecurities are barriers of instabilities of thoughts programmed in the mind of a woman. The unstableness of a woman plagues her confidence and herself worth, thus creating road blocks in the marriage. Instead of her adding worth and value, she subtracts through multiple distractions causing her husband to continuously reach back to pull her up that she may function as his splendor and not the likeness of a squalor. The husband should always reign as king in his home and marriage, what is a king without the presence of his crown. If the crown has lost its radiance it can never shine as the jewel she was created to be. The woman who never knows who she is, can never become what she intended to be.

These are the virtues that constitute a good wife, and why the husband obtains favor from the Lord.

Chapter 5

The power of identity "The Husband"

When God breathed life into the nostrils of man, he blew in him the very attributes of Himself, thereby creating man to possess the very qualities of God. This is one of the reasons why wives are to submit and honor her husband as unto the Lord, as this is done it's honoring the very essence of God. The quality of a God man is insurmountable, there is no exchange, and there is none greater no other life form in the universe is superior to that of a man. Because man houses such great qualities his responsibility is held to a higher level.

This does not negate or diminish a woman, for man was God's first line of contact, but residing inside of man was woman and as God breathed into man woman became a host to facilitate and she too became qualified to carry out the plans of God.

> *"Husbands, love your wives, just as Christ also loved*
> *the church and gave Himself up for her, so that He*
> *might sanctify her, having cleansed her by the*
> *washing of water with the word, that He might*

present to Himself the church in all her glory, having
no spot or wrinkle or any such thing; but that she
would be holy and blameless. So husbands ought also
to love
their own wives as their own bodies. He who
loves his own wife loves himself."
- (Ephesians 5:25-28)

Adam's role was to draw Eve to himself, the same as the ecclesia is drawn to Christ by the Father

[44] For no one can come to me unless the Father
who sent me draws him to me....
- John 6:44 (TLB)

Husbands have that same ability and mandate to evoke their wives unto themselves. Adam's role was to allow her to know his love and his protection, and identify that she was now sanctified to him. On the spiritual side, this is what Christ does for the Church, and what husbands are to do for their wives.

The Holding Pattern

There is a silent longing in which women need, to be wrapped in the arms of her husband, this is a natural position being that woman was taken from the rib of man. She was not extracted from his foot to be walked upon, nor was she obtained from his head to be ruler over man. But the delicate position in which she was taken was a place beneath his arms. A place that a woman naturally fits, this becomes a place of security, a place of peace, a place of tenderness, a place to be held.

It is the husband responsibility to draw her unto himself, but thank God the man it's not left to himself to complete the task. The natural pheromones of the human species has drawing power in itself, while it may appear to be odorless its strength is in its ability to attract and evoke sexual behavior of the opposite sex. So there you have it men, stretch for your arms and reel her in, you have been built with help.

Whenever a man reaches inside of his natural capability to soothe his wife, he naturally taps into the secret of her desire. Most women do not have a desire for strife, but due to the lack of understanding of a woman's design, there will almost always be the appearance of struggle between the two.

The silent message she is sending is a longing to be held, comforted, and drawn back to the place where she was once securely fastened, his ribs. What appears to be a tantrum is actually a longing. Many men mistakenly identify this as an arguable woman, or nagging wife, or nuisance, or a wife who is needy, but it's the natural position in which a woman was removed. When the husband taps into the secret of a woman he will tap into the success of his marriage. She's not always seeking for a fight, it's her inability to express her longing that needs to be fulfilled and the fulfillment is in the arms of her husband. Question, if there has been a lack of intimacy could there also be a lack of holding?

Husbands know your wife

> [7] *in the same way, you husbands must give honor to*
> *your wives. Treat your wife with understanding as*
> *you live together. She may be weaker than you are,*
> *but she is your equal partner in God's gift of new life.*
> *Treat her as you should so your prayers will not be*
> *hindered.*
> *- 1 Peter 3:7 (NLT)*

Giving honor unto the wife

Honoring her by becoming her protector and support, the husbands' position is to maintain and provide for his wife. Honor involves a deep respect coupled with love for her. There is an intensity of maintenance that a wife needs, a level of upkeep is necessary. Maintenance is an ongoing process to ensure the marriage is functioning at the highest altitude possible. It is the responsibility of the husband to know his wife and what is needed in order for her to be at her optimal which ultimately he benefits. If it's a break, a date, a backrub, a day off, a day of pampering it's the husband requirement to know. The need to satisfy the wife must stem from the depth of the covenant between God, himself and his wife.

When something or someone is honored, it's cherished and held at a high regard, handled with care, it's enjoyed, and one carries out the terms of the covenant, there's not a question of will you, *you will.*

A husband should always strive for the betterment of the wife's livelihood. As a provider his number one focus is the environment in which his gift resides. Every stage of your living is different, but there should always be visions for a new growth dimension. The starting position should always be the ceiling which becomes the floor in the next dimension. Never should you settle at the place of your beginnings. Dangerously noted is that some men move no further than the first dream or plan which is due to the aide of slothfulness. Whenever a husband does not continuously move, it causes frustration in the wife, because a body can go no further than its head, if the head refuses to move it results in stagnation which is the foul smell of procrastination. Beginnings are just that, beginnings which acknowledges that something is to follow, the only way one reaches a new beginning is that something has reached its prior destination

As every beginning becomes new, your floors become the learned experience and the place of stability from the lesson learned which makes your relationship sure, it becomes your teacher, the old transcends into the new. Never discredit the old because without it the new dimension could not come forth.

Honor a way of living

Honor the wife as—the weaker vessel—meaning she's more delicately constructed, lacking particular skills or abilities to accomplish certain things. The wife processes distinctive qualities that a husband desires and need; beauty and delicacy. This does not imply that the wife is so delicate that she is fragile; underneath her delicacy is her ability to accommodate her husband as his helpmate which radiates into her outward beauty. The husband in turn has what the wife wants his courage and strength. Together they work hand in hand and by these things God has made equality between the man and the woman, that there might be no one greater in superiority than the other.

God designed the woman to be weaker in some things, so that she could suit the marriage in her appropriate role.

> [1] *Wives, in the same way be submissive*
> *to your husbands...,*
> *- 1 Peter 3:1 (NIV)*

Submission is a word that can make or break a marriage, most women cringe at the thought of a man having authority over them, and some men boast that a man have authority over a woman. Submission not properly understood could lead to disaster in a marriage!

Submission is a willingness to yield one's actions, control and power to another without resistance. Also it means to subject oneself or allow oneself to be subjected under the power or decision of another. This does not take away the identity of the wife it enhances the quality of the wife.

Submission is a requirement. God has commanded it because, in His infinite wisdom, it's the best arrangement for a happy, fulfilling marriage. Subjection does not lower the position nor define the wife as inferior to the husband. The fact remains that the husband and wife are heirs together in Christ.

Submission has to do with order and authority, Christ Himself became a servant and submitted to God's will. There is nothing degrading about submitting to authority or accepting God's order. If anything, it is the first step toward fulfillment, fulfilling the original plan and purpose for existence.

Submission brings opportunity, an opportunity for what? For God to be glorified and the unsaved husband sanctified. If one needs to be won to Christ it will take submission as a key factor, this powerful key will unlock any locked door and gain entrance to influence the life of the husband and change the atmosphere in a home. This key *is not* to be used to manipulate the husband to give into the desires of the wife, no this key acts as a portal to the heart and soul of the husband whereby softening his heart towards a healthy relationship which ultimately The Lord gains access. A wife will never convert a husband through nagging, nor preaching, this strategy only presents an opportunity for the husband to leave the home and give attention elsewhere.

There is beauty in submission a husband finds beauty and pleasure in a wife who is willing to lay aside her demands to meet his needs. A home with lack of submission is a home of disrespect, disrespect brings contention, and contention opens up to strife, strife invites hatred and where there is hatred there is no love, where there is no love you find no beauty *only dread.*

Husbands have four areas of responsibility in relation to their wives:

1. **Natural** -to dwell with the wife, this intends that the husband provide for the physical and material needs of the home. This does not mean that the husband only should work, but it's the husband who should provide and the wife's number one responsibility should be to care for the home.

2. **Logical** - dwell with her according to understanding. It's the mandate of the husband to know his wife's moods, feelings, needs, fears, and hopes. His ears must be tuned in to listen with his heart and impart meaningful communication with her. A disturbing reality is when two people joined in marriage can live together and not really know each other! Lack of knowledge is dangerous in any area of life, but it is especially hazardous in marriage. Can a husband demonstrate concern for his wife if he does not understand her needs or problems? When a husband admits that he never knew his wife felt a certain way, is a confession that there is a disconnection that has taken place somewhere in the marriage. Fortresses are walls that are built to keep something in or something out, if in a marriage one spouse is hesitant to be open or reveal their true feelings they begin to build a wall which later turns into a fortress to protect themselves. Instead of utilizing communication as a bridge to close the gap, one refuses to express themselves which cause the bridge to be used as a way to escape inwardly, ultimately causing a sudden implosion resulting in the outward

explosion. It's what you don't say that can destroy the marriage. The home should have such a protective atmosphere of love and submission that both the husband and wife can both agree to disagree and still be happy.

3. **Expressive** – husbands giving honor unto his wife. All wives wants to be treated as though she is special, the queen in her husband's life. The husband must take the initiative in expressing his love and loyalty to his wife that creates the impression of blissfulness in her eyes. Yes, she is acknowledged as the weaker vessel, meaning not mentally, morally, or spiritually, but rather physically, with exceptions, of course, but usually speaking, the man is the stronger of the two when it comes to physical accomplishments. The husband should treat his wife like an exclusive, gorgeous, delicate ornament, which houses a precious treasure. It's a legitimate gift given to him with purpose in mind.

In the beginning of relationships, the dating stage usually the man is courteous and always thoughtful. He hangs on to all the words she say, he holds the doors, always on his best behavior, her impression of him is important. Somewhere after the courtship as he enters into the engagement, his expression becomes deeper as his love has intensified the exasperating thought that she has agreed to be his wife he explodes with joy inside. He'll do all that's in his power to make her happy as they embark on the journey to explore life together as one.

But soon after the wedding, many husbands forget to be loving, patient and gentlemanly and begin taking his wife for granted. He slowly forgets that joy in a home is made up of many *small* things, including the tiny courtesies of life. These little considerations mount up to major platforms that arouse the affection of the wife.

Silently the wife develops resentments, vast resentments often grow out of tiny hurts. Both the Husband and wife must be honest with each other, admit hurts, and seek for forgiveness and healing. Husbands to give honor to your wife, does not mean giving in to her. A husband can disagree with his wife and still esteem and honor her. He may not agree with her opinion, but he respects them. The marriage is meant to be balanced in a way that the husband needs what the wife has in her individually, and she equally needs his good traits.

4. **Spiritual** -that husbands prayers be not hindered. Prayer is one of the most essential ingredients for a good healthy marriage, but not all marriages that are good are based on prayer. For the marriages that do not have the foundation of prayer and have a good strong marriage what a blessing you have. But the greater blessing should rest on the marriages whose foundation is prayer. The indication of the atmosphere in the home is revealed through the prayer life of the couple, a home full of prayer is usually a home full of peace.

If the atmosphere of your home is off, then altitude of your prayer will be lost.

When the wife shows submission and the husband consideration, they create and inspiring encounter called marriage.

How each perceives their role in marriage will always be a factor in the relationship. Perception is key…

A key gives you access, it secures and give you control into the entrance of someplace, let's call this place a realm. The realm is one's territory of special knowledge or responsibility, such as the couple's marriage. In the marriage they both live in that realm together. Both have equal access, but both have their individual use of keys. What may be perceived as pertinent by one may not necessarily be significant to the other.

This revelation must be understood in order to reason with both parties, the reflection of each perception maybe as the result of the retraction from different angles. Example; the raising of children, the husband may have been brought up in a stern household and believes in discipline, while the wife was raised in a care free house and believes in allowing the children to live with freedom and ease. Both the husband and wife will inspire to raise the children from their paradigm which is as a result of their perception. This can cause friction in the marriage, but does this imply permanent damage? Not at all, it requires a little adjusting to bring about balance. The eyes of perception may be dimensional with reason, when one sees from one dimension and the other another there must be a coming together with reasoning until the road meets. Then and only then will access to a successful dimension be acquired.

Thou shalt not lose!

The looser is the one who chooses **not** to give in the marriage, when both parties give their best the marriage then becomes successful. What one gives they get to keep, what you fail to give you lose forever.

There are rules that govern every action in life such as, "for whatsoever a man soweth, *that* shall he also reap". They key word here is "that", for if you sow that, you get that. In other words if you give "love", love shall you receive. If you deliver confusion, confusion will be shipped back to you. It's just this simple, a person is entitled to that which they give out, and that same person has no entitlement to what they never give and stands the chance of jeopardizing and loosing what they have.

Giving does not only consist of monetary gifts, no, giving goes beyond meager spending. Giving reaches into respect, time, patience, kindness, love, laughter, motivation, emotional support, and the list goes on. Selfish is the spouse who chooses not to give.

A successful marriage is a marriage in which both spouses gives, the more one gives the greater chance it is for them to receive. Giving is a principle thing. One cannot be reluctant to give in fear of losing anything. Lost comes as a result of not giving at all.

Chapter 6

The Greatest Mistake

When a person says "I do," they are actually saying I'm starting a process of removing self-centered independence, and exchanging the "I do" to "we do". After the wedding, Married people have to go through what we call the "see it through" period. This is the time period where couples starts with the motto, "we do".

If this transition is never achieved and understood between them, their language will never change from "I do" to "we do" mentality all will continue doing everything alone. This is a major turning point in any relationship. Between the husband and the wife, the load that both individuals once carried becomes lighter because their load is evenly divided. For example, what felt like fifty pounds of weight carried alone, now feels like twenty-five when the weight is evenly distributed.

This is a learned process, where we break old habits and take time to recreate new ones. To learn a new habit is a crucial task because the subconscious mind reasons with the conscious mind of a person, instructing them to do what they know, and are willing to do. The problem is this mindset has become a stronghold which will only build walls around the progress of your marriage.

If the foundation of marriage amiss, whatever is built on this foundation will also be unsuitable and things will go wrong. Until something causes a new paradigm to shift, the old paradigm will remain. When thoughts of old habits are ushered out, the thoughts of new habits come in.

One pure thought

Sixty-eight seconds of sustained pure thought can change an old habit formed in the mind.

When one's mate is allowed to discuss hidden desires that they once were not allowed, it then creates a new foundational thought. There are new possibilities, new potential, and then a marriage is a renewed and rebuilt again.

When "I do" transitions to "We do". A marriage can excel by accomplishing what the couple strives to achieve together. However, a mistake is never view as a mistake, until the lesson is revealed; at the entrance of a revelation darkness dissipates.

When you enter a dark room and turn on the light, darkness has to excuse itself, everything hidden will be revealed. Dissection is needed to ensure proper revelation, when one miss-takes their mate he/she for-sakes their joy. Let's shed light.

When we *miss*, conveyed in this instance as overlook, or fail to spot, fail to notice, neglect, or ignore our mate; we *take* or rob them of the opportunity that could lead to ultimate fulfillment. When a spouse refuses to allow their mate the chance to bring fulfillment into their life, the marriage stands the possibility of being housed in darkness, where there a void of revelation to access their mate. If revelation is missed, the marriage will suffer the mistake of true fulfillment.

Once the mistake made, it is important to avoid repeating the same mistake. A mistake can be forgiven, but the repeat offender of the same mistake never realizes or understands the power of forgiveness and the power of that forgiveness did not become the teacher of that mistake. "I do" sometimes means "I do" make mistakes, however "I do" care enough to not make the same mistake again. Some of the greatest mistakes are the greatest miracles waiting to be recognized, thank God one can see a mistake and the miracle it's pregnant with.

Chapter 7

The Yolk don't fit

¹⁴ Be ye not unequally yoked together with
unbelievers: for what fellowship hath righteousness
with unrighteousness? and what communion
hath light with darkness?
- 2 Corinthians 6:14 (KJV)

When one person's idea in handling finances differ from the other, it will yield a hardship. The union of two people with different belief systems will cause conflicts in the marriage, unless compromise is instituted.

Marriage in itself can be a complicated union, because of the many variances of life. When different beliefs are joined together, it creates a bigger tension. This scripture is not given here to be a burden, but is to shed light of truth to aid in understanding. Most of the struggles in marriage are because of ideas, and beliefs of each individuals. As stated earlier, a person's idea of raising children could be different from the other.

This is why Paul states that one spouse could draw the other in another direction. The question that comes to mind is which direction one will go. This type of union might weaken the commitment, where integrity or standard of a person of faith is bending in compromising to appease the other, which will ultimately weaken the strength of a believer. Unless the compromise is in mutual respect of the others belief, still one is free to his or her own conviction.

This results in an unbalanced marriage that's not in proper alignment. An unequally yoked marriage will certainly have its tension until compromise is initiated. In compromising, it does not mean that one has to surrender over a person's rights or beliefs. This means that one must respect the other's right to believe, without intruding.

Example One: The husband does not share the same belief as the wife. He is a free-spirited person, who enjoys life abundantly and his wife does not (this does not include adulty, or any act that could damage the marriage). In compromising, he would **not** insist his wife joins him in activities against her convictions. Instead, he would engage in these activities, while the wife is not present. Consequently, he is still able to do what he feels expresses his enjoyment of life, which does not include his wife without jeopardizing their marriage, or way of living. In addition he does it in suitable proportions of time, always keeping in his subconscious thought, his wife.

Example two

The wife can have a strong belief in God and the husband does not, she becomes a nag to him if she always insists on him attending worship with her.

> *[1] Wives, fit in with your husbands' plans; for then if they refuse to listen when you talk to them about the Lord, they will be won by your respectful, pure behavior. Your godly lives will speak to them better than any words.*
> *- 1 Peter 3:1 (TLB)*

A believing wife submits to Christ and to her husband, that develops a gentle soft spirit will never have to fear. The Lord will look over her even if her unsaved husband creates tribulations and difficulties for her.

As a wife, the church should never be used as a leverage against the husband. A wife should never make the church building her home, while spending countless days or hours of service in *that* house while *her* house is in need. Her time of worship with the body of believers is important and necessary, she attends her regular fellowship and keeps in her subconscious mind the needs that must be fulfilled at home. This keeps the wife balanced that she never over extends herself without communicating with her husband.

The husband should never be made to feel as if he has to compete with God, there is no competition in God. Wives must understand that while she's in the presence of her husband. Her speaking in tongues is not the method of communication that he wants to hear, for everything must be placed in their proper place.

Husbands and wives; it's important to know that as believers, you do not have to impress on the other what they should believe. Living your life in front of the other will lead the way. Too often, people try to change people into what they think they should be, instead of living their life as a good example that their life would invoke a change. Let your light so shine so others may see the good in you and glorify the Father.

When both understand "compromise" it makes for a better marriage. One does not have to surrender their rights; they just understand perspective. This does not mean that an unequally yoke marriage can't work; it can work if one chooses to make work it, you may just have to work bit harder.

These are not grounds for divorce for those marriages have this dynamic:

> [12] *I (not the Lord) say to the rest of you: If any Christian man is married to a woman who is an unbeliever, and she is willing to live with him, he should not divorce her.* [13] *If any Christian woman is married to a man who is an unbeliever, and he is willing to live with her, she should not divorce her husband.* [14] *Actually, the unbelieving husband is made holy because of his wife, and an unbelieving wife is made holy because of her husband. Otherwise, their children would be*

unacceptable {to God}, but now they are acceptable to him. [15] But if the unbelieving partners leave, let them go. Under these circumstances a Christian man or Christian woman is not bound {by a marriage vow}. God has called you to live in peace. [16] How do you as a wife know whether you will save your husband? How do you as a husband know whether you will save your wife? [17] Everyone should live the life that the Lord gave him when God called him. This is the guideline I use in every church.

- 1 Corinthians 7:12-17 (GW)

The power of decision is one worth making, remember the choice you make today is the one you will live with tomorrow.

Chapter 8

The Burnt Impression

M ost people enter in the holy state of matrimony on a chimerical impression, which the focused is imaged on a fairytale, or make- believe wedding -to- be. Truthfully, there is a covenant being shared with a real man or woman who may or may not share the same ideals on marriage. Unless there is a paradigm shift in the mind of one or both, the marriage can suffer a cataclysm state due to misunderstanding.

It is vitally important before someone say "I do" that they are aware of the other's true ideals of marriage. The apprehensiveness from a spouse is due to the impression burnt into his or her subconscious mind.

A person becomes what they are taught, what they understand to do, believe their reality, and respond according to their knowledge. Any marriage can suffer because of nescience, but it is imperative that each gain the necessary awareness of what the other's pre-notion is on marriage.

Some couples are not compatible with the other. Their view of marriage is can differ. Two people can love one another immensely, but share different views. Do they need to fall out of love with one another? The answer is no. Moreover, they learn how to disagree and find the equal medium that works for their marriage to produce the best for both.

How to Find Middle Ground

A couple must learn the likes and dislikes of their spouse, learn the behaviors, what makes them happy or content, what are the trigger points that cause strife. Discern what he/ she complains about and respond accordingly. This means that if the spouse has an issue with any given thing, then the other should make all attempts to work with their spouse to resolve those problems to make ease for both parties.

Example: if it's a pet peeve for the wife not to sit in cold toilet water during a mid-night release. The husband should make all attempts rectify the matter (put the toilet seat down). This will alleviate mid night arguments.

Example: if the husband's pet peeve is toothpaste left on the counter with the top off, the wife should find a solution to that problem. This will cease the early morning duel.

Hey Listen Up

Listen up! Our sense of hearing enables us to hear and interpret the sounds in the world around us. Thanks to our ears, we can hear waves crashing on the shore, our favorite songs on the radio, and the alarm clock ringing in the morning! The following discussion will help a couple to understand that through the volume levels set during intense negotiation couples may engage in, sometimes called arguments; they can preserve and protect their marriage by developing a keen sense of hearing. Another method in which to hear is the human spirit, once sounds enter into the ear- gate, it then travels into the mind that has its residency in the soul realm. If there are any impurities of any kind in the mind, will, or emotions of the person, it will latch on to the sound that is traveling through channels as it penetrates through. The human spirit will accept or reject, then respond and send the signals back through the channel, where the response will be positive or negative.

Every part plays a role in the response, so it is imperative that each person keeps the gateway open for a clear transmission. Sometimes, people need to clear out old wounds of the past, before they become road blocks of the present. For example have you ever heard an old song and it reminded you of something or someone in your past. This sound has a direct link to a particular emotion, which is imbedded in the subconscious mind. This song could make you respond by crying, laughing, or even smiling, which is a direct result of the emotion connected to the sound. Couples should learn to sit down and have open discussions with their mate to assure conflict resolution have been reached on past problems.

Marriage Discussion Questions for both the husband and the wife

1. Is it important that my spouse and I hear one another?

2. When we listen, how does it benefit us?

3. Am I listening to my spouse?

4. Are you in tuned with the parts of our body help you listen?

5. When your spouse is communicating with you, can you identify his or her sound of disgust?

6. How does that sound make you feel?

7. What are your least favorite sounds your mate makes? Why?

When things get heated get out of the "volume contest"

After spending hours in the studio writing, producing, and being involved in the mixing process of music sometimes the music volume level had to be decreased in order to hear the finer nuances within the mix. Sometimes the session had to be canned for that day, because of what producers call "tin ear" this is where everything in the mix begins to sound the same, and the human ear can't separate distinct sound. The only thing left is to leave the studio, go home and come back the next day with fresh ears in order to be effective. The ear is the most important tool used in the mastering music process and also in the music industry. One common trick in the industry is to deceive the ear by making the music louder, louder can cover up, but louder is also noise, don't be deceived by the noise; noise is almost always for the worse. Music is mixed and mastered at the highest and loudest frequency and that frequency is really called distortion however the human ear cannot detect it all the time "They make it loud to get listeners attention," Are the arguments in your marriage suffering from ear fatigue? Are your words able to be heard by the human ear? Are your words robbing your marriage of its emotional power and leaving your mate with ear fatigue? These are the questions. It may be time for all of us to stop the "volume contest", raise the white flag of surrender during the "loudness war" and create a new atmosphere where the volume level is at a decibel level where we can really hear what is being said from our mate as opposed to what we think we hear in the distortion.

Chapter 9

Table It!

--------•⌒⌣⌒•--------

*³ He that kept his mouth kept his life: but he that
openeth wide his lips shall have destruction.*
- Proverbs 13:3 (KJV)

*³ Self-control means controlling the tongue! A
quick retort can ruin everything.*
- Proverbs 13:3 (TLB)

How often has marriages crumbled due to the lack of self-control, couples has forfeited their covenants by treasonable words they have spoken to the one they pledged their love to. Words have power they possess the ability to tear down and destroy all human intelligence with a simple syllable.

In the heated atmosphere of an argument one shouts the word "hate"; that single word can tear at the heart of the other leaving un-repairable damages which may very well be handed down for generations to follow. We are what we learn; we become what we are taught; and we teach what we know. Most often the manner in which a couple handles disagreeable situations is a result of learned behavior.

A word of wisdom to all married couples; never involve other people in your conflict resolution unless it's a qualified source, such as a pastor or marriage counselor. Your loved ones love you and most often they will have a bias opinion of the situation. When personal information is shared to those other than your spouse or qualified people, their personal view can obstruct the truth.

 This in the long run can hinder the progress of healing, if and when healing can occur the outside source has been left with the imprint of negativity of your spouse. Word to the wise; "if you let the bird out of the cage, chances are you will be left with an empty cage". Meaning, some things are to be left in the personal home, once things are release to the wrong ears, it then becomes transmitted in the atmosphere of confusion which will boomerang back as destruction to your home. There is an old saying that holds some truth to it, "one man trash is another man's treasure". You very well may be sharing your spouse personal issues "trash" to the one person who perceives it a "treasure". Now you have just opened the door for the bird to find rest in the nest that perceives it as treasure, every listening ear is not a sound worth listening too. Remember everyone has an opinion, but is every opinion needed?

Table talk means there is a mutual place in the home that is used for nothing else except resolutions.

Rules to govern by:

1. To Begin:

The spouse who begins the conversation is the one who sanction for table it. This is done solely by the spouse who throws in the white card, (this does not by no way insinuates that the one who throws in the card is right or wrong, it means that someone was mature enough to stop the moving pain) Each spouse will take their turn in expressing their feelings in a calm and even tone manner. Both have equal minutes to talk and to listen, while one is talking the other is listening *only*, the listening spouse should write down all rebuttals and never blurt out anything, wait until it's his or her turn.

2. Respect each other:

While at the table both spouses agree to be respectful and to be open to hear each other's side. Both agree to be honest, kind and never talk out of turn or call names. The couples never use derogatory terms and never use such phrases as; "you always, or you never" for these are phrases that point a continuous finger at the other and most certainly will cause the other to turn defensive. For the spouse will quickly adapt to a sense of uselessness and tune the other out.

3. The Subject at hand:

The conversation must at all times be about the situation at hand! Never is the couple allowed to back track to prior situations, keep the main the main. Simply put if it happened last week and it wasn't addressed last week then it's out of play.

4. **Every conclusion must result in resolution:**

    If the resolution is we agree that we disagree on the subject then do it with the commitment to respect the other's opinion. Here is an example to bring clarity; the husband dislike the big purple hat that his wife loves to wear when they are together, this causes arguments every time, but the hat makes the wife feel strong and dependent how do they agree to disagree? First the husband has a right not to like the hat and the wife has the right to want to wear her hat, this settles the fact that both have rights to their opinions. The manner in which to settle and bring both happiness and respect, is to allow the wife to wear her hat but she agrees to never wears it when she's with her husband, this way she has her cake and he can eat too. Everything has a resolution! It's a matter of love, respect and comprising on both sides.

5. **When resolution is reached the couple is free to enjoy hot passionate love making.**

    Arguments or intense disagreements causes the body to react, the heart beats faster to pump more oxygen, adrenaline and sugar into the bloodstream. Blood pressure begins to rise and the muscles in the body intensify, in other words your body is now ready for action! Why not give the body what it needs, *a release*! The more intense the disagreement the more intense the sexual pleasure, so go on enjoy yourself, But only after the completion of steps one through four.

Items needed:

a. Table (preferably unused for anything else)

b. 2 chairs of equal height as not to intimidate

c. Timer

d. Pad

e. Pencil

f. Respect

g. Love

h. Patience

How to arrive at the table:

At the onset of a disagreement one of the two should stop the conversation kindly with gestures as; Hey let's table it or this may not be the right time for this, can we continue this in a few minutes, will you meet me at the table, etc. Or the spouse can retrieve the table it card and present to their spouse. Note: these gestures should not be presented in a sharp arrogant way! It must be done in meekness with purpose to resolution. Once one spouse has made such a gesture the other spouse must immediately come into agreement. Note: one should not make the convening time at an unrealistic time, such as the other may have an appointment, or on their way to work, this should be done in a reasonable time.

In the beginning it may seem awkward and unreasonable but the outcome will be effective. Communication is the key to a great marriage.

Chapter 10

Indicators

Check the Engine Light

If your vehicles emergency check engine warning light indicator suddenly appears lit on the console of the car, it would be an indication that your car needs maintenance. Your vehicle has been electronically wired to indicate that there is a problem that demands your immediate attention. Marriages have certain necessities for maintenance as does your vehicle, where there are no tune-ups in the marriage, that marriage will trigger emergency light indicators. What happens when the check engine light comes on in a marriage? An example: if the answer is to see the light and choose to do nothing about it, then one must except that continuation in such manor is to ignore the possibilities of trouble in the marriage! If one chooses not to ignore the possible engine problem with one's vehicle then why jeopardize losing a life mate? Which has the greater value attached? The marriage should be viewed as a precious commodity, whereas no amount of monetary values compares. Your love for your spouse in your marriage is priceless!

This is a thought-provoking area for every marriage, ask yourself this question; have you made your marriage a priority, or are you waiting to see the engine light come on? Both men and women have engine warning lights that only the spouse can satisfy. If her intimacy needs are not satisfied or she feels depleted the light will come on, on the other hand signals will be released indicating his testosterone is in need of service.

Indicator lights

Non- verbal communication is as much an indicator light as an argument," silent withdrawal" is as damaging as the "let it all out "argument. The questions are when was the last time a full diagnostic test was conducted in a marriage, does the marriage still have life, or is it barely thriving? Indicator lights show up in the least expected ways, sometimes trouble light indicators become visible when there is lack of interest in general conversations once shared between two people, lack or loss of creativity and aggression concerning the things that were once enjoyably shared by both, and now there's little to no input in the participation of decision making that use to be prevalent in the spouse. Last but not least the late night headaches which leads to no romance, all these are indicator lights. If you notice that, lately, that the spark that was once observed in your mate's eye is missing, check the indicator lights!

Is the touch the same? Is the look the same? Is your connection the same?

Each spouse must make sure if they are the mechanic *male or female* chosen to check the indicator light, then check it frequently, if not your marriage may be on the verge of having problems. Selah (*pause and think of that*).

Your Reaction can make the difference

There is sending then there is receiving. How one respond to any given situation can either make it or break it. It's usually not the sending that ignite the flame it's the response to what was sent that does. One can choose to react or not to react; the right reaction can cause the right results. Not saying a thing is not the solution, it will cause a sudden implosion one day which the destruction will have a worst effect than that of an explosion. You can say what you mean without being mean.

Going within one self and ignoring the situation is not the answer. No one wins when there is no attempt to pursue. To have and to hold till death parts is interpreted as: *I promise to pursue whatever it takes to keep you happy, to meet your needs. I promise attempt every challenge with my heart fixed on we will win together. I promise even when the road gets rough to find a smooth patch and extend from there. I promise that I will gather the pieces that shatter your heart and find a way to mend them. I promise to see a mistake as missed opportunity and not hold you captive as a prisoner in my thoughts. I promise to wait beside the gate of your heart with expectancy that your heart will always have a place just for me!* What God has put together let no man put asunder, that includes the two of you!

Marriage has often been entered in too lightly, with no thought of the repercussions to the vows that one so easily dismisses. The vows spoken in marriage are recorded in heaven the rain doesn't wash them away; the clouds do not cover them. But like the rainbow after the storm is lifted it appears as a reminder of the words of a covenant. Like that rainbow no matter how severe the storm it appears as a reminder of a covenant of love. Marriage is a covenant that should not be broken.

It remains to be seen

Many times the focus needs to be re-adjusted and brought into reality due to what is perceived as negative physical traits.

 When a man first meets a woman something inspires a reaction in him thereby causing him to respond; whether his response engages him to comment about her beautiful hair, her perfectly adorned attire, the brilliance of her mind, the success of her future, along with her exceptional physical appearance. These were qualities that he enjoyed, gaining the attention of those around as they entered a room or just strolled along, she shined as though she was a perfectly fashioned diamond for all to admire. This man valued her partnership at the conception of their relationship, acknowledging to his friends and to the entire world that he would always esteem her and he respected her above any other woman. Spoken from his mouth and before a great cloud of witnesses, that the commitment to his life mate was for better or for worse, forsaking all others to be with her 'til death do they part. An alarm has be sent as a reminder of what was in the heart, mind, body and soul on that special occasion of unity.

This same woman whom he quietly laid besides during the night, is in fact the same woman who true loved was pledge to one day. All that she once was she still can become today and even greater if he could only embrace the total package and not just a piece of her past. Could it be possible that his image of her is seen through a dim glass which has limited the true picture of his wife. If only the scales would fall off he could tap into the essence of her being and she could become the apple of his eyes again. Maybe she hasn't changed at all but only the perception of her. Could it be that in the beginning the attraction and arousal were for superficial reasons, if the reasoning was not just surface level he would have entered into the marriage understanding that "physical appearances sometimes change"

Perhaps it's been forgotten who bore one or more of his seeds, being stretched until she brought forth the king or the queen that he so desired. It's the selfless transformation of her body which still bears the permanent marking caused by the stretching of herself to bring about a part of him that should never be forgotten. The heart filled pain is when he questions whatever happened to her, a statement which takes heartless nerves.

The man would start to experience struggles within himself because he secretly have been addicted to his mate's physical outward being however there could possibility have been or he has lost the attraction to her emotional and spiritual being. On an emotional level she could have been hurting and deprived for a long time, but how could he know, the only thing he has seen was her physical appearance.

Is it possible for a man to look beyond a self-engaged idea to reach inside to catch a glimpse of her emotional wellbeing, if this could ever happen he would find that time was lost and stimulation shut out causing missed opportunities for him to impregnate her mind with his word and thoughts to satisfy her need to be valued as a helpmate.

There is a yearning inside of a woman a need to be more than just a show piece but to become all she was created to become, she is waiting to conceptualize dreams and visions and to birth purpose and fulfill destiny. When this is not realized by a man he misses the most admirable qualities of a woman.

Readjustment

The husband becoming one with wife is the only way to tap into her spiritual and emotional being. A factor to him becoming one with her is predicated on him knowing her and dwelling with her according to knowledge. Failure to understand or satisfy her needs, the husband has hindered his prayers. Look at this scripture again.

> *In the same way you married men should live*
> *considerately with [your wives], with an intelligent*
> *recognition [of the marriage relationship], honoring*
> *the woman as [physically] the weaker, but realizing*
> *that you] are joint heirs of grace (God's unmerited*
> *favor) of life, in order that you prayers may not be*
> *hindered and cut off. [otherwise you cannot pray*
> *effectively]*
> ***- 1 Peter 3:7 (AMP)***

When a husband takes time to know and understand the spiritual and emotional needs of his wife then focus on them, becoming as important as his sexual needs that husband would find inside her the jewel that she is. She is much more than just a physical being – her mind is sexy, her emotions are alive, her spirituality is waiting to be touched by the *god man* that is on the verge of emerging. Physical appearance may sometimes change, but the girl, locked on the inside of her never does. Tonight could be the night, tonight this same husband could walk up to his wife and embrace her, kiss her, celebrate her for the efforts and sacrifices she has made for their family.

Today can be the day for reconnection for what God has put together; man has allowed to be torn apart. This could be the time every ill spoken word becomes a distant fading memory, because his passionate kiss. This could be the day that he wakes up and realize that physical appearances change, but the inside woman he married will always remain the same. If she was good enough to marry, she is good enough to stay with and celebrate for the rest of their lives.

DIMENSION THREE
"Rekindling the Flame"

Chapter 1

Take it all off

OUTSIDE LOOKING IN

The church is reserved from teaching what the world is willing to and has been perverting for centuries and decades! But it's time to be real with this generation to save the next! Be real, tell the truth take it all off.

The ideals of sexual intimacy have been burnt into the eye gate invading the subconscious mind, ultimately this effects ones true expression of sexual intimacy. Premarital sex is believed to be the way of life, with no understanding of its repercussions. Humanity has been programmed contrary to its original intent (the Bible) concerning premarital sex, so when it's time to be join in holy matrimony the thing that was intended to be enjoyed is often shunned away to an isolated state of frigidity! In marriage the doors of sexual excitement are somehow closed and on lock down at the time that it should be open and full of life. Notice the imbalanced person how free sexually they were prior to marriage then after the wedding day change occurs. The reason is this; the gateway to sexual intimacy was intended only to be opened and enjoyed after marriage. When it is prematurely opened through sexual intimacy it creates a soul tie. That soul tie leaves an unholy door open that remained open in the subconscious mind. Why? Because the people involved have formed an illegal alliance which is seen as covenant in the spirit realm.

For this reason a delay or set back in the natural formed. When the season came to fulfill God's original sexual intent through marriage one had nothing left to give, because the person gave their sacred offering at the wrong time. Don't worry all is not lost for one can redeem the time lost! But it must become a desire and one must be willing to work for it, by breaking the unholy alliance and committing themselves to their new covenant partner.

One of the problems needing to be addressed is the teachers. Some of the instructors are living in the closed box of "it's not proper to discuss this matter." All while marriages are suffering from lack of knowledge.

Now is the time in your marriage that you should be experiencing all the openness and the joys of a fresh fling with the spouse that God has given you. These are the best days to be transparent through open communication about what your needs, wants and desires are in the bedroom, breathe! The church is about to step into position, taking its rightful place back and teach sexual intimacy without fear and intimidation. Marriages have been suffering in silence. But, that's the real problem, suffering in silence, living the lies of secrecy; in our opinion, spirits of fidgety are secret struggles. Why not talk about it, it's time to be relieved of the infection and bring about healing to the marriage. Couples put on their public faces, attend their public churches, work their public jobs, shop in their public stores, But live in their private pain all because no one wants to expose the truth. There is suffering and neglect in the bedroom, where lack of intimacy creates barriers, that lead to frustration then bitterness creeps in. These negative emotions may produce a house of strife. When a house is left in this manner, unattended, this house will become a dwelling of contempt.

Chapter 2

Two is Enough

A dultery is a violation of the covenant given before God that constituted the marriage and also can break the marriage bond. However, sexual sins against the marriage bond can be forgiven, and the husband and wife can implement forgiveness and make a new beginning.

Sexual sins are severe because they undermine the institution of family life and the oneness of the marriage relationship. This grieves God in such a way that He compares idolatry to adultery because of the resemblance of the divine-human and husband-wife relationships. When the family tranquility and unity is destroyed, the spiritual life and worship falls as well.

> [4] *Marriage is honorable among all, and the bed*
> *undefiled; but fornicators and adulterers*
> *God will judge.*
> **- Hebrews 13:4 (NKJV)**

The bed is undefiled. The word "UNDEFILED" *means that the bed is unstained by sin,* there is no sign of filth caused by outside sources, and it has not be contaminated or corrupted from the original intent and covenant.

Closeness and intimacy are gifts from God. There is the resemblance of the church, which is a church filled with the love and passion coupled with a relationship with Christ. *Intimacy* is the relationship between a husband and wife stimulated by a desire and need. Pure worship in fellowship with Christ prevents the unholy union with dark forces, ultimately leading to broken covenant. God hates adultery because it's like a relationship with Satan at the same time, the covenant is not broken only with the spouse, the covenant is broken with God.

When there is passion along with intimacy in bed between husband and wife, it should prevent any unfaithfulness in marriage. The marriage bed is the one place where covenant is reestablished, rekindled, restored, reignited and not restrained! There is absolutely no place for another person in the marriage bed, not in word, thought or deed.

> [18] *Flee from sexual immorality. All other sins a man commits are outside his body, but he who sins sexually sins against his own body.* [19] *Do you not know that your body is a temple of the Holy Spirit, who is in you, whom you have received from God? You are not your own;* [20] *you were bought at a price.*

Therefore honor God with your body.
- 1 Corinthians 6:18-20 (NIV)

Illicit sexual behavior breaks fellowship all over again with God, with each act. The act of fornication is not true worship unto God, for the Father is seeking those who worship Him in Spirit and in truth. His presence is where covenant is honored-the marriage bed. Therefore, sexual intimacy in the purpose that God intended between husband and wife introduces the pleasure of being one with the Father.

Communication is key

Discussing the sexual needs is a very delicate matter, and should be handled in the gentlest manner. It's not what you say that can hurt its how and when it is said, that does. A spouse should always consider the feelings of the other, without neglecting their own concerning sexual needs. Because it is a very sensitive matter, it should never be discussed in the moment of contention. The choice of time and words should be thought out carefully with a desire towards a unified resolution.

The husband or wife is aware that there are some differences between them both, however this can work as an advantage or disadvantage. As an advantage, it enables one to initiate a compassionate conversation concluding in a positive result. But as a disadvantage what can be resting in their subconscious mind that could lead to a heated debate. The wrong words at the wrong time can cause more stress and possibly damage the other. Timing is everything, while spending time to arouse your mate by gentle touches, caressing and holding is a better time to express the needs *than* while one is in the midst of an important task, or the moment in anger. The wrong time will cause despair and provoke a negative response. When this happens trust is lost and may never be regained. The fact is the husband or wife desires to please the other, never let them away. A soft word can turn away strife.

Time is love and love is time

Time invested in sensual intimate moments sharing love is time never wasted. The time investment will yield the greatest return to those who refuse to allow life's many distractions to sabotage what should be years of happiness. While a second of time is lost, will eventually amount to years of lost and wasted occasions that could have been maximized through effective time management one second at a time. Time is the unspoken voice that never needs to be heard, but it does need to be seen, felt, and given away to another in order that the recipient's emotional response might be transformed into something tangible that can be directly correlated to the investment of time. When both emotions are transmitted then tangible happiness will manifest. The proof will be that the time invested will leave a mark on the receiver for life throughout the rest of their lives. If your time is important to you, give it to your spouse, you will find out how important your time is to them also. If you truly love, take the time to deposit into your mates love bank. Make the time to talk, and to date time is a choice that one makes a decision on how they will use it.

Chapter 3

To have and to hold

A *man without a wife is like a tree missing its branch*
In the garden, God's original intent was that they would both be naked and free from shame. The weather was perfect; their skin glistened from the sun, the reflection of the moon rest on the waters, creating the perfect atmosphere for romance. Exploring the gift of intimacy was as natural as the rising of the sun, for there was not the burden of shame. Why, because sin had not entered the earth, for shame can only arise from sin consciousness. Whenever the consciousness of sin is prevalent, it invites the power of shame, which will cause one to not walk in the freedom that was intended by God. Marriage is one of the antidotes against shame, because in marriage sex is honored and intended to be enjoyed.

Marriage provides the God-given right to experience the pleasure of sex and to produce children. The Lord commanded man and woman to be fruitful and multiply, and fill the earth. This does not in any way imply that sexual intimacy is only for procreation, for there are people who marry and never have children, because of various reasons. However, the bearing of children has an importance in the marriage union. Many would say that the act of producing children is pleasurable and they are correct. We are sexual beings and pleasure plays the greatest part intended for enjoyment. One of the utmost desires of humanity is sexual intimacy. Sadly, there are numerous couples who lack in sensual gratification. The time is now to begin to explore the pleasures in which was meant for humans to enjoy in marriage.

One engine over heats while the other never gets hot

Both the husband and wife can differ in their sexual needs. One spouse may require sex more frequently than the other. Sometimes, this is because of the age cycle where men and women peak at different ages. It is said that a man reaches their highest point of sexual activity in his early twenties, while the woman typically peak in her mid-thirties to forties. It would be easier if we all peaked together!

Because of this transition, one spouse may not be totally satisfied while the other is. Instead of the couple communicating, emotions are bottle up inside and can turn into anger or strife if not dealt with immediately. It's not that the one spouse is not sensitive to the need of the other spouse, instead they do not know how to communicate or adapt to change they are enduring. Communication is the key, openly discussing ones needs and desires is imperative in the marriage. Together a couple can find ways of creating new levels of sexual pleasure so that both can climb the mountain and slide down together. This is a matter of coming out the box, what may have worked in the earlier years may not work in the now years. It's a matter of synchronizing new love patterns and pleasures to create a new dimensional symphony. Simply put, find new ways of pleasing one another.

Chapter 4

A Little Spark Will Ignite A Fire

Rekindle means to regenerate, revitalize, rejuvenate, rebirth, replenish, restore, repair [7]

There is no time such as the present to begin to rekindle the flame, "If it has a little spark, then it has a lot of possibility". When two people focus with one mind, on the same thing such as reviving or renewing feelings of love interest, then new energies will begin to submerge. Thoughts have power, when both share the same thoughts especially at the same time, in the same room heat then produced. Human Possess the power of thought to obtain what it desires. If one desires an intimate moment with their spouse, it can be achieved, for the power is in the thought. If one thinks they are sexy, they will become sexy. If that same person believes they are not, they will produce the effects of that thought. If there is a need to rekindle the passion in the marriage, there must be a deliberate change in their thought. Man is what he thinks, and he becomes what he believes. He is limited by his own thoughts.

---

[7] Thesaurus: English (United States)

The power of knowing self! If one can shift their paradigm to think, they are ***only one*** touch away from being able to change the moment from chaos to peace, happiness to romance because it is all in the way one thinks. Time out from negative thinking, since one gets what one expects.

Thoughts have power to draw on negative thoughts and will release negative energy. So instead of tonight thinking negatively, think hot and sexy, the longing of pleasure, that the flame that lost its spark is about to be relight. It's a matter of exchanging the previous cold thought for the hot steamy one as the sparks from the mind will set the vibrations in the room. Intimacy begins with a thought. The precise thoughts produce the exact effect. Tune up the atmosphere for a hot romantic night, think about it. When the music of love and touch plays in harmony, the night begins to flicker with hope and restoration. Hope is the igniter, once two people ***decide*** that they can make the fire burn again. The flicker of a spark can become a blazing flame of love, because love is the strongest emotion. Let the band play on!

It's a matter of stimulating the senses

There are five senses within the human body. These senses are sight, touch, hear, taste, and smell. Each sense has a purpose and is stimulated by different factors and motivations, but all five connect with the human body to distinctive degrees. No two function alike or have similar effects, but when all five are being stimulated simultaneously, it causes the body to react in an overwhelming expression called orgasm. If sensitivity to any of the senses has been lost, one of the others will increase to accommodate that need.

Finding new and greater pleasures requires re-engaging the senses.

1. Visual stimuli may require a few adjustments such as creating an atmosphere of visual pleasure. This can include decorating the bedroom, changing the color from the old season color to a deep passionate color. Add new sheets, curtains, and pillows to the bed to create a love haven for the two of you. Get rid of and your bedroom of clutter, baby toys, and work paraphernalia, dim the lights, add candles.

   Wives visit the store that shares the secret to unlock the mysterious side of you. Every wife has a secret fantasy she longs for her husband to explore; it's the visual stimulant that becomes eye candy that engages the husband. This may require a woman to create a different image even if it's in her mind. "as he thinks in his heart, so is he (Proverbs 23:7)." How one sees herself is how her husband will see her too! Think sexy and become that image!

   Likewise husbands may be need to change the "boxer shorts" from the old ones to eye pleasing new ones. Some husbands are lacking in knowledge that wives are visual as well. Taking time to invest and update can spark a little flame. Whoever said that women don't need to be turned on! A well-oiled triceps is more pleasing than the old rusty one. Women like to glide over their men's body too; it makes changing positions a little easier!

2. Touching is a need for *every "body"*, the human body was created to respond to touch. Exploring other areas on the body of your spouse can open a new window of opportunity for intimacy. Both the husband and the wife have a longing to be caressed. The gentle rubbing of the knees or fondling with the ankles or stroking of the hair line, gently touching the frame of the lips, the palm of the hand, can send warm signals to the brain which starts arousal. Notice the word gentle, beginning and continuing with a soft slow rub, the mind should be clear focusing only on the area of the body being explored. Time needs to be set aside, and the atmosphere set, this is not for the quickie on the way to work. Explore, excite, and explode together! Try adding body massage oil to the touch, a little heat aids to the fire.

    It is imperative that each spouse make an extra effort to develop soft smooth skin free of abrasive rough areas and unsightly ash. Good proper skin care and hygiene is a must to heighten the arousal of touch whether it's giving or receiving!

    The market is full of bath products such as oils, sugar and salt scrubs great for the nourishment of skin making this a part of a daily routine would aid in the pleasure of touch. Becoming good to ones on body add to the benefits of delight.

3. Sound what an awesome instrument the ears are! Sounds send vibrations of waves in the atmosphere which draw one's attention in. Music is a stimulant that increases pleasure, listening to the right sounds will put one in the mood. There are some musical keys that relate to the human anatomy, playing the right music stimulates the body. It is said that playing soft music in the letter "C" which relates to the blood, genitals, and muscles is good for healing of the body, so let the sexual healing begin. Try new music together such as classical and soft jazz, choose you music carefully, the wrong notes can bring about a different result. Permeating your bedroom with the right sounds can positively affect your attitude, altitude and energy. Music soothes even the savaged of beast, he Tarzan and she Jane, synchronized together in one passionate sound.

4. Oh taste and see that the love is good. Chocolate and strawberries are known to be aphrodisiacs, spice up your love life while enjoying great taste as well. Try natural eatable body lotions and crèmes as stimulants of pleasure. Wives, if chocolate is your fix find some chocolate body paint and take your appetite out on him! There is a taste for every pallet, husbands snatching off the panties worked at one stage, but eating off the panties works at every stage. Visit your local adult store together, find out what works for your marriage.

5. Leave the jungle outdoors unless of course the jungle is your pleasure! The scent of a woman never leaves his mind, investing in the right fragrance will always stimulant his

thoughts. The pheromone of a woman grabs the attention of a man and becomes a calling card for romance. Light up your bedroom with sensual aromas that entices intimacy. Rid the bedroom of the dirty hamper, the smell of sweaty shoes and envelope the room with the fragrance of passion.

Sexual intimacy is to be a time of pleasure and reciprocal satisfaction for both the husband and wife. It should never be looked upon as drudgery or work, for it is the coming together and exchanging of pleasure with only one goal, total gratification for both and glory unto God. In other words it is not good or justifiable for one to reach the height of ecstasy and leave the other hanging from the edge of the mountain top!

"A healthy marriage is one whose foundation is friendship, honesty, and commitment, therefore intimacy lives beyond sexual pleasure."

There's healing in the bed

Again the bed represents covenant in the initial covenant the Lord has with His children He promises to be Jehovah Rapha, our healer. The bed is a healing salve for the marriage! No matter what the problems or issues when the husband and wife unite as one in the bed, deliverance will come, if they desire for it. There is healing for a marriage in sexual intimacy. One may notice that; the most intensive sexual passion is usually after the couple have experience a trauma, whether it was an argument, death, or some type of crises. When they join together in sexual union it relieves the tension, redirects the emotions, and once again strengthens the marriage. The one room that's the couples most sacred in the home is their bedroom, that's the reason special care should be given to that room. The most important furniture that the couple can ever purchase for their home is their *bed*. Many people spend more time and money in the furniture that is out in the open for others to enjoy, but the emphasis should be on the one place that no one is allowed to enjoy but the husband and his wife, unfortunately very little emphasis is put in this area. Why stimulate the senses for other people, and refuse to stimulate the senses for your intimacy. The greatest investment is the one that brings restoration, comfort, excitement, pleasure, and joy. The bed sets the tone for the entire home; make the best investment in the one place that brings healing for the marriage *"the altar of marriage covenant"*, **the bed**.

The place that a person tends to go to when they are sick is the bed, the greatest example is found in the way that children desire to climb in their parents bed especially if they are sick, become afraid, need nurturing, or are feeling insecure. Notice where children tend to go first, the one piece of furniture they love to dwell in it's their parent's bed. Why, because healing flows from that bed.

The magnitude of the bed in marriage cannot be overstressed. God's Word says that it is so important that the husband and wife are not to separate for any period of time apart from fasting and prayer and even then separation is not to occur unless it is by mutual consent. Understanding that both are to be in agreement with the length of time of due to fasting, one spouse cannot choose alone to enter into separation of intimacy without consent of the other. After all the husband's body is not his own and neither is the wife, there should always be a shared agreement.

Sexual intercourse is part of the physical illustration of love within a marriage and provides emotional closeness; it intensifies the couple's friendship, and love for each other while strengthening the oneness of the marriage. Sexual intimacy should not be taken lightly or shared with just anyone, because a part of each person is release to their partner. Emotions are being exchanged, souls are becoming one...

"Keep the marriage bed sacred and the bed will keep the marriage."

Chapter 5

A spiritual awakening

The Garden

The moment the husband enters inside his wife something transpires beyond ones imagination this begins in the invisible realm. Much focus is on the physical or natural sense of sexual intercourse but there lays an incredible experience that goes beyond the act.

[10] How beautiful are your expressions of love, my bride, my sister! How much better are your expressions of love than wine and the fragrance of your perfume than any spice. [11] Your lips drip honey, my bride. Honey and milk are under your tongue. The fragrance of your clothing is like the fragrance of Lebanon. [12] My bride, my sister is a garden that is locked, a garden that is locked, a spring that is sealed. [13] You are paradise that produces pomegranates and the best fruits, henna flowers and nard, [14] nard and saffron, calamus, cinnamon, and all kinds of incense, myrrh, aloes, and all the best spices. [15] {You are} a spring for gardens, a well of living

> *water flowing from Lebanon.* [16] *[Bride] Awake, north*
> *wind! Come, south wind! Blow on my garden! Let its*
> *spices flow from it. Let my beloved come to his*
> *garden, and let him eat his own precious fruit.*
> ### - Song of Songs 4:10-16 (GW)

Note the expressions of Solomon the woman is compared to a *garden*, a paradise of freshness, and she is *the bride* (the wife) who acknowledges that she has a *precious garden* sweet to the taste and welcomes him to her garden!

In the beginning it was the woman who was extracted from the man, now, it is man that **enters** into the woman. As he enters into her womb, it's as though he has re-entered *the garden*, this is a familiar place to him, a place created just for him. Eden was a dimensional realm of warm pleasure and delight. Eden was also the place that God created for man, the home of God. The garden holds the key to the delight of the eye and the sweetness of taste. No matter the color, or shape, it brings a delight! The natural fragrance that flows from Eden delights the senses of man. In the center of the garden is the tree of life, where healing flows. It is said the more sexual intercourse one engages in, the healthier one becomes. The tree of life was placed in the midst of the garden intentionally as a symbol of that life which man should ever dwell, provided sin does not corrupt that original plan. Preservation for the body of man flows from her garden, causing a continual energy vital to man.

The garden is man's euphoria, producing feelings of happiness even at the thought of visitation to the garden, which causes stimulation in him. God's goodness is shown in His purpose of the garden. The features of Eden clearly shows that God cares deeply for man, for it produces four components essential for man of which are provision, multiplication, restoration, and healing. These aspects all flows from the garden. Sexual intercourse has been stated as having health benefits such as boosting the immune system: good for the heart, aids in longevity of life, decreases depression, and other studies demonstrates its benefits.

Overall, the benefits of sexual activity for humans is joy, and happiness. The garden shows that God designed the ideal place for man's residence and was planted by God Himself. The Garden is just not a physical dimension; it is also a *spiritual atmosphere*, of *a spiritual ambiance*. It's intense beauty and provision was created to give man a sense of awe and worship, stirring a praise and thanksgiving from man to God. This deliberate masterpiece was admirably fitted to keep man consistently in mind of God; only God could create such an environment that would manifest an intense pleasure that would bring Him glory! Sexual intimacy takes a person to a state of adoration for the creator. He gets pleasure out of seeing His creation (man) receiving pleasure; who knew that God would do all this just for marriage.

It is worship to God! Dating is likening the outer court. Foreplay likens the inner court. Sexual intercourse is entering into the Holy of Holies, just like re-entering in the Garden of Eden in which God Himself prepared for man to dwell and had intimate communion with God. For this reason alone, the marriage bed should remain undefiled. This is in comparison to the priest that enters into the Holy of Holies and if sin enters in, he would die. One cannot enter the presence of God with the stench of sin, and expect God to be pleased and accept their worship.

> *³ Who can climb Mount God? Who can scale the holy north-face? ⁴ Only the clean-handed, only the pure-hearted; Men who won't cheat, women who won't seduce.*
>
> **- Psalms 24:3-4 (MSG)**

Sexual intimacy is for both the husband and his wife that is one of the highest forms of pleasure to humanity. When the husband enter into his wife, in her garden, she welcomes his presence with the warm excitement of celebration as this encounter re-establishes the two becoming one flesh.

Special care should always be given to the garden, the husbands mandate is to dress and keep the garden. Cherish the gift of the garden, and the garden will welcome the gift of the man.

Intimacy and worship

Just as worship is an essential asset in the relationship between man and God, so is intimacy as significant in the marriage. The marriage bed is the only sexual bed honored by God, because **that bed** represents covenant.

God gets pleasure in our worship unto Him. Passion is expressed through the crimson-colored blood of Christ as He hung on the cross. In worship unto Him, His presence is felt and experienced in a way that cannot be explained. The sound of our praise and adoration welcomes Him to come closer and dwell with us. The music gets His attention as the melody chimes Him Holy. The smell of our sacrifice reaches the highest heaven, which becomes an invitation of joining one in the inner court. The sweet taste of His presence leaves one wanting for more. This is true intimacy where worship is the ultimate experience, and where passion meets pleasure.

When a husband and wife join together in a passionate experience, the presence of God fills that room. Intimacy and worship goes hand and hand. The sexual encounter of the husband and wife is likened unto the worship experience with God. It's personal, life- changing, pure, untainted, and fulfilling, there are no room for third parties. It is *only* the two of them, as two people become one flesh.

This is the revelation between The Spirit of God and His church.

The wife is like the Holy Spirit, and the husband like the Word. When the Word penetrates the Womb of the Spirit – a Spiritual explosion happens. When the Word and the Spirit unite together, it is the full manifestation of the power of God. Sexual intimacy is the one experience God created with covenant that the two in marriage can enter in together with Him **as one**.

www.ingramcontent.com/pod-product-compliance
Lightning Source LLC
Chambersburg PA
CBHW072150020426
42334CB00018B/1937